STEP·BY·

GREEK
Cooking

The Family Circle Promise of Success

Welcome to the world of Confident Cooking, created for you in the
Family Circle Test Kitchen, where recipes are double–tested by our team
of home economists to achieve a high standard of success.

MURDOCH BOOKS®
Sydney • London • Vancouver

BASIC GREEK PANTRY

Most of the ingredients for Greek cooking are available at your local supermarket and delicatessens. Fresh herbs, lemons, tomatoes and spring onions are the staple ingredients found in almost every Greek household.

Bread: Bread is served with every Greek meal, often used to soak up any sauce, oil or juices on the plate. Loaves are traditionally round with a light coating of flour.

Cheeses: Feta, kasseri, kefalotiri and ricotta are commonly used cheeses. Feta is a soft, moist white cheese made from ewes' milk, creamy sometimes crumbly in texture. Kasseri is a medium-hard, strongly flavoured yellow cheese with a rind pressed into the shape of a cylinder. Kefalotiri is a firm, dry, salty yellow cheese with a tough rind moulded into the shape of a skull.

Eggplant: Also known as aubergine. Large firm vegetable with a purple almost black skin is used in moussaka and many other dishes.

Filo Pastry: Paper-thin sheets of pastry made from flour and water, used for both sweet and savoury dishes.

Garlic: The most favoured ingredient used fresh in Greek cooking is available all year round. Some dishes are so strongly flavoured with garlic that the dish can become quite piquant to the taste.

Greek Coffee: Also known as Turkish coffee, it is very finely ground to a powder. The coffee is combined with water and sugar and cooked over a flame in a cylindrical pot with a pouring lip called a "briki". It is heated until it just reaches the boil and a thick froth has formed and served in demitasse cups accompanied by a glass of iced water.

Herbs: Oregano, thyme, mint and parsley are used fresh and dried in Greek cooking.

Lamb: The most popular meat used in Greek cooking. It combines well with almost any herb, spice, fruit or vegetable. Lamb is particularly complemented by olive oil, lemon, garlic and oregano.

Lemons: Used to flavour sauces, soups, dips and syrups, to marinate and tenderise meats, and to garnish meat, fish and poultry dishes during and after cooking.

Octopus: Baby octopus are used for pickling or pot cooking. Do not salt octopus as this will toughen the flesh. Larger octopus are less tender and need to be pounded with a mallet, marinated for several hours or overnight before being grilled or barbecued.

Olive Oil: The most versatile ingredient and most commonly used in Greek cuisine. Use a light olive oil for deep frying and the dark, heavier olive oil for cooking or flavouring dressings and dips.

Olives: Kalamata olives are the most commonly used today. They are black, firm-fleshed, slightly sweet olives ideal for salads, and cooking.

Ouzo: Colourless, aniseed-flavoured spirit, traditionally served in small straight-sided glasses, often mixed with a little water.

Pulses: Brown lentils, chick peas, black-eyed beans, broad beans, canellini beans and lima beans are commonly used in Greek cooking. They are added to rich tomato-based sauces to make soups or casseroles, or simply mashed into a dip with oil and lemon juice, or served cold as a salad with a dressing to taste.

Semolina: Both fine and coarse ground semolina are used in sweets and cakes.

Spices: The main spices used in Greek cooking are ground white pepper, cracked or whole black peppercorns, ground or bark cinnamon, whole cloves and allspice.

Taramasalata: A highly flavoured dip usually made from cods' roe, olive oil, lemon juice, mashed potato or soaked and squeezed dry stale bread.

Tzatziki: Traditional yoghurt dip made with thick yoghurt, grated or chopped seedless cucumbers, garlic, fresh herbs, salt and pepper.

Vine Leaves: Available from supermarkets and delicatessens in packets, fresh young leaves are used. Soak vine leaves in warm water and rinse well before using to remove excess salt.

Yoghurt: Firm, plain natural yoghurt is always best for dips and cooking.

3

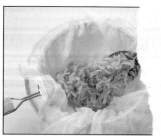

Line a fine strainer with cheesecloth. Spoon cucumber in.

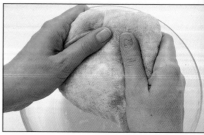

Squeeze firmly to remove moisture from cucumber.

STARTERS & SOUPS

Delicious savoury snacks and dips are perfect for party food or as an introduction to a Greek meal.

Tzatziki

Chilled yoghurt dip, highly flavoured with garlic.

Preparation time:
15 minutes
+ 2 hours
refrigeration
Cooking time:
20 minutes
Serves 6

---

3 large Lebanese
    cucumbers, coarsely
    grated
500 g thick natural
    yoghurt
3 cloves garlic,
    crushed
1 teaspoon finely
    chopped fresh dill

1 tablespoon olive oil
salt and freshly
    ground black
    pepper, to taste
2 pitta breads
2 tablespoons olive
    oil, extra

---

1 Line a fine strainer with cheesecloth. Spoon cucumber into strainer, cover with cloth to enclose.
2 Press and squeeze firmly to remove the moisture from the cucumber. Place cucumber into mixing bowl.
3 Add yoghurt, garlic, dill and oil; mix well. Season to taste. Cover with plastic wrap; refrigerate 2 hours or overnight.
4 Preheat oven to moderate 180°C. Cut through centre of pitta breads with sharp knife. Brush rough side with oil. Cut each round into eight wedges. Bake bread on ungreased tray 20 minutes or until crisp. Serve cool with chilled yoghurt dip.

Add yoghurt, garlic, dill and oil; mix well to combine.

Cut through the centre of pitta breads with a sharp knife.

Taramasalata

This classic Greek dish is a favourite all over the world.

Preparation time:
  20 minutes
  + 2 hours
  refrigeration
Cooking time:
  20 minutes
Makes 1½ cups

---

2 large old potatoes, peeled	*⅓ cup lemon juice*
120 g cods' roe or tarama	*⅔ cup olive oil*
	2 tablespoons fresh parsley

---

1 Cut potatoes into 2 cm cubes. Place into small pan; cover with water. Bring to boil, reduce heat and simmer, covered for 15 minutes or until tender. Drain. Mash potato with fork until almost smooth; cool.
2 Using electric beaters, beat roe in small mixing bowl on high speed 2 minutes. Add potato gradually, beating thoroughly after each addition.
3 Add juice and oil gradually, beating thoroughly after each addition. When all the oil and juice has been added, beat mixture on high speed 5 minutes or until light and fluffy.
4 Refrigerate for 2 hours. Finely chop parsley. Transfer purée to serving dish; sprinkle with parsley. Serve at room temperature with bread and olives.
Note: Store dip in an airtight container in refrigerator for up to 1 week. Bring to room temperature before serving. Serve Taramasalata on bread or use as a dip with raw vegetables.

HINT
For added flavour, finely grate an onion and squeeze juice into the dip; discard onion pulp. Potatoes can be replaced with four slices of stale white bread, crusts removed, soaked in water, squeezed dry.

Mash cooked potatoes with a fork until almost smooth.

Using electric beaters, beat roe. Add the potato gradually.

When all oil and juice have been added, beat until light and fluffly.

Finely chop parsley; sprinkle over taramasalata.

Potato and Onion Rissoles

Little savoury snacks.

Preparation time:
30 minutes +
1 hour standing
Cooking time:
12 minutes
Makes 30

---

1 large potato, peeled	*1 teaspoon dried*
1 large onion	*oregano leaves*
500 g minced beef	*1/3 cup coarsely*
1 tablespoon brown	*chopped continental*
vinegar	*parsley*
1 tablespoon tomato	*1/2 teaspoon ground*
paste	*white pepper*
1 egg, lightly beaten	*salt, to taste*
2/3 cup (about 50 g)	*1/3 cup plain flour*
dry packaged	*1/3 cup olive oil*
breadcrumbs	

---

1 Coarsely grate potato and onion into a large mixing bowl.
2 Add mince, vinegar, tomato paste, egg, breadcrumbs, herbs, pepper and salt to taste. Knead mixture for 3 minutes until ingredients are well mixed. Cover with plastic wrap, refrigerate 1 hour.
3 Shape 1 tablespoon of mixture at a time into balls. Flatten and taper the ends slightly. Coat rissoles lightly in flour; shake off excess.
4 Heat oil in pan. Cook rissoles in small batches over medium heat for 3 minutes each side or until golden and cooked through. Carefully remove rissoles from oil with tongs or a slotted spoon. Drain on paper towels; keep warm. Repeat with remaining rissoles.
Note: Coarse mince is best for this recipe. Using finely ground mince may result in a smooth yet sticky mixture to work with. Add more breadcrumbs to the mixture if this happens.

Coarsely grate potato and onion into a large mixing bowl.

Using hands, knead mixture for 3 minutes until well combined.

Shape into small balls. Flatten and taper the ends.

Cook rissoles in small batches until golden brown. Remove with tongs.

Dolmades

Serve as entrée or finger food at parties.

Preparation time:
1 hour +
1 hour standing
Cooking time:
50 minutes
Makes about 35

---

250 g vine leaves in brine
3/4 cup olive oil
2 large onions, finely chopped
3/4 cup short-grain rice
6 spring onions, chopped

1/3 cup coarsely chopped fresh dill
1 tablespoon finely chopped fresh mint
salt and freshly ground black pepper, to taste
1 1/2 cups water
1 tablespoon lemon juice

---

1 Rinse vine leaves in cold water, then soak in warm water 1 hour; drain. Heat 1/2 cup oil in small heavy-based pan. Add onions. Cook over low heat 5 minutes; remove from heat, stand covered for 5 minutes.

2 Add rice, spring onions, herbs, salt and pepper to pan; mix well. Lay out a vine leaf, vein-side up.

3 Place 3 teaspoons of mixture onto centre of leaf. Fold sides over mixture then roll towards tip of vine leaf. Repeat process with remaining filling and leaves.

4 Place five vine leaves over base of medium heavy-based pan. Arrange rolled dolmades into pan in two layers; drizzle with remaining oil. Place a plate on top of the dolmades; cover with water. Bring to boil, reduce heat and simmer, covered, for 45 minutes. Remove plate; drizzle with lemon juice. Serve warm or cold.

Note: Fresh vine leaves can be used in this recipe if available. Use small leaves, blanched briefly in boiling water.

Heat oil in small pan. Add onions and cook for 5 minutes.

Add rice, spring onions, herbs, salt and pepper to pan.

Place 3 teaspoons of mixture onto each leaf. Fold sides over and roll up.

Line pan with vine leaves, arrange dolmades and cover with a plate.

Cheese Triangles

Crispy filo treats.

Preparation time:
35 minutes
Cooking time:
20 minutes
Serves 4–6

---

200 g feta cheese
100 g ricotta cheese
1/4 cup grated
* mozzarella*
* cheese*
1 egg, lightly beaten

white pepper, to taste
15 sheets filo pastry
2 tablespoons olive
* oil*
2 tablespoons butter,
* melted*

---

1 Preheat oven to moderate 180°C. Place feta into medium mixing bowl; mash with a fork. Add the ricotta, mozzarella, egg and pepper, mix well.
2 Place one sheet of pastry lengthways onto work surface. Brush all over with combined oil and butter. Fold into thirds lengthways.
3 Place 1 tablespoon cheese mixture onto corner of pastry strip. Fold this corner over the filling to edge of pastry to form a triangle. Continue to fold until filling is enclosed and end of pastry is reached. Repeat process with remaining pastry and filling.

4 Place triangles onto lightly greased oven tray. Brush with oil and butter mixture. Bake 20 minutes or until crisp and golden.
Note: While working with filo, keep pastry covered with a clean damp cloth to prevent the sheets drying out. Cooked cheese triangles can be frozen for up to 3 months. Reheat before serving.

HINT
Finely chopped fresh herbs, such as parsley, dill, thyme, basil or rosemary can be added to this recipe if liked. Sprinkle triangles with 1 tablespoon sesame seeds before cooking.

Mash feta, add ricotta, mozzarella, egg and pepper and mix well.

Brush one sheet of pastry with oil and butter. Fold into thirds lengthways.

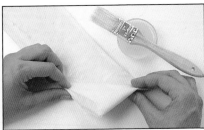

Fold pastry over filling to make a triangle, and fold to end of pastry.

Place on prepared tray and bake until crisp and golden.

Stuffed Whole Eggplant

Small eggplant filled with spicy tomato.

Preparation time:
15 minutes +
30 minutes
standing
Cooking time:
1 hour
Serves 6

3 small eggplant (not slender)	*salt and freshly ground black pepper, to taste*
1 tablespoon salt	*2 tablespoons freshly chopped parsley*
1/2 cup olive oil	
2 cloves garlic, crushed	*2–3 tablespoons lemon juice*
3 medium onions, thinly sliced	*1/2 teaspoon sugar*
4 ripe tomatoes, chopped	*1/3 cup water*

1 Cut stems from eggplant and cut in half lengthways. Cut a long deep slit into each eggplant half, leaving 1.5 cm at each end. Sprinkle eggplant with salt.

Place in bowl of iced water. Stand 30 minutes. Drain, squeeze dry with paper towels.
2 Heat half the oil in frying pan. Add garlic and onions.

Cook over medium heat for 5 minutes or until onions are soft. In a bowl combine onions with tomatoes, salt, pepper, and parsley. Mix well.
3 Preheat oven to moderately slow 160°C. Heat remaining oil in pan. Cook the eggplant over medium heat until lightly browned. Remove from pan. Place in ovenproof dish. Spoon onion mixture into slits. Add the combined juice, sugar and water to dish. Cover and bake for 45–50 minutes, basting occasionally with pan juices. To serve, sprinkle with parsley and spoon over cooking juices.

Cut a deep slit lengthways into each eggplant half.

Place onions in a bowl with tomatoes, salt, pepper and parsley. Mix well.

Cook eggplant over medium heat until lightly browned.

Place eggplant in dish and pour in combined juice, sugar and water.

Tomato and Brown Lentil Soup

Preparation time:
  10 minutes
Cooking time:
  40 minutes
Serves 4

1 large onion	*2 small dried chillies*
1 cup (200 g) brown lentils	*1 bay leaf*
1/4 cup olive oil	*1 litre water*
1 clove garlic, crushed	*salt and freshly*
1/4 cup tomato paste	*ground black pepper, to taste*

1 Finely chop onion. Rinse lentils in cold water; drain well.
2 Heat oil in a large heavy-based pan. Add onion and garlic, stir over low heat for 10 minutes.
3 Add tomato paste, chillies, bay leaf, lentils and water and bring to boil. Reduce heat, simmer, covered, for 30 minutes or until lentils are soft.
4 Remove chillies and bay leaf; discard. Add salt and pepper to taste. Serve with crusty bread, garnished with fresh red and green chillies.
Note: This dish can be made up to 2 days ahead. Store, covered, in refrigerator and reheat just before serving.

Use a sharp knife to peel and finely chop the onion.

Add onion and garlic to pan, stir over low heat for 10 minutes.

Add tomato paste, chillies, bay leaf, lentils and water to pan.

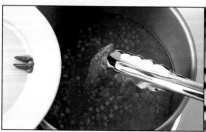

Remove chillies and bay leaf from the soup and discard.

Separate lettuce leaves and wash and drain thoroughly.

Slice cucumber, radishes and onions. Chop tomato.

SALADS, RICE & VEGETABLES

These dishes can be served as a main course, or as side dishes, in smaller quantities.

Greek Salad

Fresh and light.

Preparation time:
15 minutes
Cooking time:
nil
Serves 4

1 coral lettuce	*2 tablespoons olive oil*
1 large Lebanese cucumber	*1 tablespoon brown vinegar*
1 large tomato	*1/2 teaspoon dried oregano leaves*
2 radishes	*salt and freshly ground black pepper, to taste*
1 small onion	
8 black olives	
60 g feta cheese	

1 Separate lettuce leaves. Wash thoroughly and drain well. Tear lettuce into bite-sized pieces, arrange on a serving platter.

2 Cut cucumber into rounds and chop tomato. Thinly slice radishes and onion. Scatter cucumber, tomato, radishes, onion rings and olives over lettuce.

3 Cut cheese into 1 cm cubes, scatter over salad.

4 Place oil, vinegar, oregano, salt and pepper in a small screwtop jar and shake well. Pour dressing over salad just before serving.

Note: Firm-fleshed black olives such as kalamata olives are best for this salad. They are available from supermarkets and delicatessens. Chopped green capsicum and anchovies can be added to this salad.

Cut feta cheese into 1 cm cubes and scatter over salad.

Combine dressing ingredients in a small jar and shake well.

19

Country Bean Salad

A hearty main course salad featuring typical Greek flavours.

Preparation time:
15 minutes +
1 hour standing
+ 1 hour
refrigeration
Cooking time:
40 minutes
Serves 4

---

1 cup (200 g) dried canellini beans
2 tomatoes
2 onions, thinly sliced
3 spring onions, chopped
1/3 cup coarsely chopped continental parsley
1/2 red capsicum, cut into strips

DRESSING
1/4 cup olive oil
1 tablespoon lemon juice
2 teaspoons finely chopped fresh dill
salt and freshly ground black pepper, to taste
5 canned anchovy fillets, drained

---

1 Place beans into a medium pan; cover with water. Bring to boil, remove from heat; leave, covered, 1 hour. Drain and rinse. Return beans to pan; cover with water. Bring to boil, reduce heat. Cover and simmer 40 minutes or until tender; drain.

2 To peel tomatoes, make a small cross on the top, place in boiling water for 1–2 minutes and immediately into cold water. Remove and peel down skin from the cross. Cut tomato in half; gently squeeze to remove seeds and roughly chop flesh.

3 Place beans into a large bowl. Add tomato, onions, spring onions, parsley and capsicum; mix well. To make dressing: combine oil, juice, dill, salt and pepper and pour over salad; mix well. Cover salad and refrigerate 1 hour.

4 Cut anchovies into long thin strips and arrange over salad just before serving.

Simmer beans for 40 minutes. Remove from heat and drain well.

Peel the skin from tomatoes; squeeze gently to remove the seeds.

Add tomato, onions, spring onions,
parsley and capsicum to beans.

Slice anchovy fillets into long thin strips
and arrange over salad.

21

Spinach Rice

Simply healthy.

Preparation time:
5 minutes
Cooking time:
45 minutes
Serves 4

90 g butter	*2 tablespoons olive oil*
1 cup long-grain rice	*2 large onions, finely chopped*
2 cups rich chicken stock	*250 g frozen chopped leaf spinach*
salt and freshly ground black pepper, to taste	*4 spring onions, chopped*

1 Heat butter in medium heavy-based pan; add rice, stir over low heat 10 minutes or until lightly golden.
2 Add stock, salt and pepper. Bring slowly to boil, stirring constantly. Reduce heat and simmer, covered, 20 minutes. Cover and set aside.
3 Heat oil in a small pan. Add onions, stir over medium heat for 5 minutes; add spinach. Reduce heat, cook, covered, for 10 minutes or until spinach is hot. Add spring onions, stir 1 minute.
4 Add spinach mixture to rice. Stir until just heated through.

Heat butter, add rice and stir over low heat until golden.

Add the rich chicken stock, salt and pepper to pan.

Heat oil and cook onions. Add spinach, cover and cook for 10 minutes.

Combine spinach mixture with rice. Stir until heated through.

Broad Beans with Peas and Artichokes

Preparation time:
  10 minutes
Cooking time:
  15 minutes
Serves 4–6

---

2 medium onions
2 tablespoons fresh
  dill
1 tablespoon fresh
  mint leaves
1/4 cup olive oil
250 g frozen broad
  beans, rinsed,
  drained
1/2 cup water
2 tablespoons lemon
  juice

250 g frozen peas,
  rinsed, drained
400 g can artichoke
  hearts, drained, cut
  in half
4 spring onions,
  chopped
salt and freshly
  ground black
  pepper, to taste

---

1 Slice onions into rings. Finely chop dill and mint.
2 Heat oil in large pan. Add onions. Stir over low heat for 5 minutes or until soft and golden.

3 Add beans, water and lemon juice to pan. Bring to boil, reduce heat and simmer, covered, for 5 minutes.
4 Add peas, artichoke hearts

and herbs. Simmer, covered, 5 minutes or until peas are just tender but not soft. Remove from heat, stir in spring onions, salt and pepper. Serve warm or at room temperature.

Note: Peeled, fresh broad beans and peas in season can be used instead of frozen in this recipe. Bottled artichoke hearts can be used instead of canned. Drain but do not rinse the bottled variety before using. Garnish finished dish with dill and mint sprigs, if liked. Serve as a side dish with a meat or fish course and steamed rice or potatoes.

Slice onion into rings and finely chop dill and mint leaves.

Heat oil, add onion and cook gently until soft and golden.

24

Add broad beans, water and lemon juice to pan.

Add peas, artichoke hearts and herbs. Stir until peas are cooked.

Tomato Rice Cups

Preparation time:
30 minutes
Cooking time:
1 hour 30 minutes
Serves 4

---

8 (1½ kg) large ripe
   tomatoes
⅓ cup olive oil
3 large onions, finely
   chopped
⅔ cup short-grain
   rice
¼ cup tomato paste

1 cup coarsely
   chopped continental
   parsley
salt and freshly
   ground black
   pepper, to taste
½ cup water
2 tablespoons olive
   oil, extra

---

1 Arrange tomatoes on a board, base side up. Cut bases from tomatoes with a sharp knife; set tops aside. Squeeze tomatoes gently to remove excess seeds; discard seeds. Use a small spoon to scoop out flesh and remaining seeds from tomato cups; chop flesh finely. Set cups aside.

2 Heat oil in heavy-based pan. Add onions, cook over low heat 20 minutes, stirring occasionally. Add rice, stir over low heat 3 minutes. Add chopped tomato and tomato paste. Bring to boil, reduce heat and simmer, covered, for 7 minutes. Remove from heat; cool slightly. Stir in parsley and season with salt and pepper to taste.

3 Preheat oven to moderate 180°C. Spoon mixture evenly into tomato cups; use reserved bases to cover filling. Arrange tomatoes in a deep baking dish.

4 Pour water into dish. Drizzle oil over tomatoes. Cover dish with foil. Bake for 30 minutes, remove foil and bake for 30 minutes more. Baste with pan juices just before serving. Serve hot.

Use a small spoon to scoop out flesh and seeds from tomatoes.

Add rice to pan with onion, stir over low heat for 3 minutes.

Spoon rice mixture into tomato cups. Top with the lids.

Arrange cups in a deep baking dish; drizzle olive oil over.

Using a sharp knife, slit the octopus head open and remove the gut.

Pick up the body and use the index finger to push the beak up; remove.

SEAFOOD

Greece's position on the Mediterranean ensures that its cuisine is rich in delicious seafood dishes.

Octopus in Red Wine

Preparation time:
20 minutes
Cooking time:
35 minutes
Serves 4

---

1 kg baby octopus
1/3 cup olive oil
1 large onion, finely chopped
2 bay leaves
2 tablespoons dry red wine

2 tablespoons brown vinegar
1/2 teaspoon cracked black pepper
1/2 teaspoon dried oregano leaves

---

1 To clean octopus, use a small, sharp knife to slit open the head; remove the gut.
2 Pick up the body and use the index finger to push beak up; remove and discard. Rinse octopus thoroughly; pat dry with paper towels.
3 Place octopus, oil, onion and bay leaves in large heavy-based pan. Cook, uncovered, on medium heat 20 minutes or until almost all liquid is absorbed, stirring occasionally.
4 Add remaining ingredients to pan. Bring to boil, reduce heat and simmer, covered, for 15 minutes or until octopus is just tender. Serve warm or cold with Greek salad.
Note: Do not add salt to this dish as the octopus is already quite salty. For a slightly sweeter, less acidic flavour add one teaspoon soft brown sugar.

Place octopus, oil, onion and bay leaves in a large pan.

Add wine, vinegar, pepper and oregano leaves to pan.

Prawns with Feta and Olives

Preparation time:
15 minutes
Cooking time:
20 minutes
Serves 4

750 g medium green prawns	1/4 teaspoon cracked black pepper
2 tablespoons olive oil	2 teaspoons fresh lemon thyme leaves
2 cloves garlic, crushed	60 g feta cheese, chopped
2 dried chillies	12 black olives
410 g can tomatoes, crushed	salt, to taste

1 Peel prawns leaving tails intact; devein.

2 Heat oil in a large shallow pan. Add the garlic and chillies, stir over low heat for 1 minute. Add the tomatoes and pepper. Bring to boil, reduce heat and simmer, uncovered, for 15 minutes, stirring occasionally.

3 Add prawns and thyme, stir over low heat 4 minutes.

4 Add cheese and olives, stir until just heated through. Add salt to taste. Remove chillies and discard. Serve with crusty bread and boiled rice if desired.

Peel the skin from prawns, leaving the tails intact; devein.

Add tomatoes and pepper to pan and simmer for 15 minutes.

Add prawns and thyme; cook over low heat for 4 minutes.

Add feta and olives to pan, stir until heated through.

Baked Snapper with Vegetables

Preparation time:
12 minutes
Cooking time:
40 minutes
Serves 4

---

1 kg whole snapper
2 tablespoons olive oil
2 large carrots, finely chopped
2 sticks celery, finely chopped
2 tablespoons tomato paste

salt and freshly ground black pepper, to taste
1 cup water
1/4 cup coarsely chopped continental parsley
1 tomato, thinly sliced
1 medium onion, cut into thin rings

---

1 Using scissors, trim the fins and tail of snapper. Wipe over the surface with damp paper towels to remove any loose scales. Wipe out the gut area with damp paper towels.

2 Heat oil in medium pan. Add carrots and celery, stir over low heat 5 minutes. Add tomato paste, salt, pepper and water. Bring to the boil, reduce heat, simmer, uncovered, 5 minutes. Remove from heat, add parsley.

3 Preheat oven to moderately hot 210°C. Pour the sauce into a baking dish large enough to fit fish. Place the snapper over sauce. Arrange overlapping slices of tomato on top of fish. Scatter onion rings over fish and sauce; sprinkle with extra salt and pepper.

4 Bake 30 minutes or until cooked. To check fish is cooked, flake flesh with a fork. It should flake easily. Serve hot.

Note: Cook this dish just before serving. The sauce can be prepared several hours in advance. Cover and store in the refrigerator.

Trim the tail and fins of snapper with scissors.

Add tomato paste, salt, pepper and water to carrots and celery in pan.

Pour sauce into dish, place snapper in pan and arrange tomato over.

To check fish is cooked, flake the flesh with a fork.

Fried Fish with Garlic Sauce

Preparation time:
  25 minutes
Cooking time:
  16 minutes
Serves 4

---

4 skinless fillets of white fish	*GARLIC SAUCE*
⅓ cup self-raising flour	*2 large potatoes, peeled*
1 egg, lightly beaten	*4 cloves garlic, crushed*
¼ cup cold beer	*1 tablespoon white wine vinegar*
⅓ cup olive oil	*salt and freshly ground black pepper, to taste*
⅔ cup breadcrumbs	*⅓ cup olive oil*

1 Cut each fillet in half lengthways and pat dry with paper towels. Sift flour into small bowl; make a well in the centre. Gradually add the combined egg and beer. Using a wooden spoon, beat until all liquid is incorporated and batter lump free.
2 Heat oil in pan. Dip fish into batter one piece at a time. Drain off excess batter, coat with breadcrumbs.
3 Cook fish in oil over medium heat for 2 minutes each side or until golden and cooked through. Remove from pan; drain on paper towels; keep warm. Repeat with remaining fish. Serve fish with Garlic Sauce.
4 To make Sauce: Cut potatoes into 1 cm cubes. Cook in small pan of boiling water for 8 minutes or until tender; drain. Place potatoes in a small bowl; mash with a fork until almost smooth. Add garlic and vinegar, mix well. Season to taste. Add oil a few drops at a time, beating constantly until all oil has been added and mixture is thick and smooth. (This may take 5 minutes.)

Sift flour into a small bowl. Pour in the combined egg and beer.

Dip fish pieces into batter; drain and coat with breadcrumbs.

Cook fish in oil over medium heat until golden brown, turning once.

Cook cubed potatoes in boiling water until tender.

Make 12 deep cuts into the lamb. Place a piece of garlic in each cut.

Place lamb in baking dish. Sprinkle with cinnamon, salt, pepper and oregano.

MEAT & POULTRY

In Greek cooking, lamb, beef and chicken are turned into very special, and often very substantial, meals.

Roast Lamb with Potatoes

Preparation time:
10 minutes
Cooking time:
2 hours 15 minutes
Serves 4–6

1.5 kg leg lamb	*salt and freshly*
3 cloves garlic, cut	*ground black*
into four	*pepper, to taste*
lengthways	*2 teaspoons dried*
1/3 cup lemon juice	*oregano leaves*
1/2 cup olive oil	*4 large potatoes,*
1 cup chicken stock	*peeled and cut into*
1/4 teaspoon ground	*eighths*
cinnamon	

---

1 Preheat oven to moderately hot 210°C. Trim lamb of excess fat. Make 12 deep cuts into lamb. Insert a piece of garlic into each cut.

2 Place lamb in a deep baking dish; pour combined juice, oil and stock all over.

Sprinkle lamb with cinnamon, salt, pepper and oregano.

3 Roast, uncovered, for 45 minutes; add potatoes. Toss to coat with pan juices; season. Reduce heat to moderate 180°C. Bake lamb with potatoes for 1 hour 30 minutes for well done. Turn lamb halfway during cooking, basting the meat occasionally with pan juices.

4 Remove from oven, leave, loosely covered with foil, in warm place 10 minutes before carving.

Add the potatoes to pan and toss to coat with pan juices.

When cooked, remove from oven. Leave for 10 minutes before carving.

Souvlakia

A practical, do-ahead dish for entertaining or picnics.

Preparation time:
20 minutes
+ overnight
refrigeration
Cooking time:
20 minutes
Serves 4

---

*1 kg leg lamb,
  boned*
*1 green capsicum, cut
  into 2 cm squares*
*1 red capsicum, cut
  into 2 cm squares*
2/3 cup olive oil
1/3 cup lemon juice
*1 tablespoon white
  wine vinegar*

*2 cloves garlic,
  crushed*
*3 teaspoons dried
  oregano leaves*
*2 bay leaves,
  crumbled*
*salt and freshly
  ground black
  pepper, to taste*

---

1 Trim lamb of excess fat and sinew. Cut lamb evenly into 3 cm cubes.
2 Thread the meat and capsicum pieces alternately onto oiled skewers, place in a non-metal dish.
3 Combine oil, juice, vinegar, garlic, oregano, bay leaves, salt and pepper. Pour over skewers. Cover with plastic wrap and refrigerate overnight, turning occasionally. Drain and reserve marinade.
4 Place skewers on lightly greased grill. Cook over medium heat 10 minutes or until tender, brushing with reserved marinade several times during cooking. Serve Souvlakia with warm pitta bread and Greek salad or Tzatziki (cucumber yoghurt dip).
Note: Uncooked kebabs can be frozen in marinade in an airtight container for up to one month. Thaw kebabs in the container; cook as directed. Soak bamboo skewers in water before cooking to prevent burning.

Trim lamb of excess fat and sinew and cut into 3 cm cubes.

Thread meat and capsicum alternately onto oiled skewers.

Combine oil, juice, vinegar, garlic, herbs and salt and pepper. Pour over skewers.

Brush with reserved marinade several times during cooking.

Moussaka

A traditional dish, uniquely Greek.

Preparation time:
20 minutes
+ 1 hour
standing
Cooking time:
1 hour 45 minutes
Serves 6

3 medium eggplants
1 tablespoon salt
1/2 cup olive oil

MINCE SAUCE
2 tablespoons olive oil
1 large onion, finely
  chopped
500 g minced beef
2 tablespoons dry
  white wine
425 g can tomato
  purée
1 tablespoon finely
  chopped fresh
  continental parsley

2 teaspoons finely
  chopped fresh mint
  leaves
1/2 teaspoon ground
  cinnamon
1/4 teaspoon ground
  white pepper

CHEESE SAUCE
90 g butter
1/3 cup plain flour
2 cups milk
2 eggs, lightly beaten
2/3 cup grated romano
  cheese

1 Cut unpeeled eggplant into 1 cm slices. Sprinkle both sides with salt; stand in a colander 1 hour. Rinse in cold water; drain well. Squeeze out excess moisture with paper towels.

2 To make Mince Sauce: Heat oil in pan. Add onion and mince. Stir over high heat 10 minutes or until well browned and all liquid has evaporated. Add wine, tomato purée, herbs, cinnamon and pepper; bring to boil. Reduce heat, simmer, covered, 20 minutes, stirring occasionally. Remove lid and simmer 10 minutes.

3 To make Cheese Sauce: Heat butter in small pan; add flour. Stir over low heat 2 minutes. Add milk gradually to pan, stirring until smooth. Stir over medium heat 5 minutes or until mixture boils and thickens. Cook 1 minute; remove from heat. Add eggs and cheese, beat until smooth.

4 Preheat oven to moderate 180°C. Heat oil in heavy-based pan. Cook eggplant a few slices at a time until golden; remove from pan, drain on paper towels. Divide eggplant into three. Arrange one portion over base of shallow ovenproof dish. Spread with half the mince sauce, second layer of eggplant, remaining mince and eggplant. Spread cheese sauce over eggplant. Bake 45 minutes or until golden. Leave in dish for 5 minutes before serving.

Slice eggplant, sprinkle with salt and leave to drain for 1 hour.

Cook onion and mince over high heat until well browned.

Add milk gradually to butter and flour mixture, stirring constantly.

Arrange layers of eggplant and mince in an ovenproof dish.

Spiced Beef and Onions

Preparation time:
25 minutes
Cooking time:
1 hour 30 minutes
Serves 4

¼ cup olive oil	*¼ teaspoon cracked*
750 g whole baby	*black pepper*
onions	*salt, to taste*
1 kg chuck steak	*1 bay leaf*
3 cloves garlic, cut in	*1 tablespoon brown*
half lengthways	*vinegar*
½ cup red wine	*2 tablespoons tomato*
1 cinnamon stick	*paste*
6 whole allspice	*1½ cups water*

1 Heat the oil in a large heavy-based pan. Add onions, stir over medium heat 5 minutes or until golden; remove from pan and drain on paper towels.
2 Trim meat of excess fat and sinew. Cut into 3 cm cubes. Add the meat all at once to the pan. Stir over high heat 10 minutes until well browned and almost all the liquid has been absorbed.
3 Add garlic, wine, spices, salt, bay leaf, vinegar, tomato paste and water to pan, bring to boil. Reduce heat, simmer, covered for 1 hour, stirring occasionally.
4 Return onions to pan, stir gently to coat with sauce. Simmer, covered, 15 minutes. Discard cinnamon, allspice and bay leaf before serving. Serve with rice, bread or potatoes and seasonal steamed vegetables.
Note: This dish can be frozen in an airtight plastic or aluminium container for up to one month. Reheat gently just before serving.
For a rich flavour, use 1½ cups of beef or veal stock instead of water in this recipe, or 1 cup of wine and 1 cup of water.

Cook onions over medium heat for 5 minutes until golden.

Add meat to pan and stir over high heat until well browned.

Add garlic, wine, spices, salt, bay leaf, vinegar, tomato paste and water.

Return onions to pan and stir gently to coat with sauce.

Beef and Tomato Casserole

Preparation time:
    10 minutes
Cooking time:
    1 hour 40 minutes
Serves 6

---

*750 g gravy beef
2 tablespoons olive oil
4 cups water
1 cup risoni pasta
410 g can tomatoes,
    chopped*

*1/4 teaspoon cracked
    black peppercorns
salt, to taste
1/4 teaspoon ground
    cinnamon
1/3 cup grated kasseri
    cheese*

1 Trim meat of excess fat and sinew. Cut into 4 cm cubes. Heat oil in pan. Add meat, stir over high heat for 5 minutes. Add water, bring to the boil. Reduce heat, simmer, covered, for 1 hour.
2 Preheat oven to moderate 180°C. Using a slotted spoon, transfer meat to a shallow ovenproof dish. Sprinkle risoni over the meat.
3 Combine 3 cups of the meat stock with the tomatoes, pepper, salt and cinnamon. Pour into dish.
4 Bake, covered, 35 minutes. Add stock or water if necessary during cooking. Sprinkle with cheese.

Heat oil and add meat to pan. When browned, add water and simmer.

Using a slotted spoon, transfer meat to an ovenproof dish. Sprinkle with risoni.

44

Pour over the combined stock, tomatoes, pepper, salt and cinnamon.

Bake until meat is tender. Add more stock or water if necessary.

Baked Beef and Pasta

Preparation time:
12 minutes
Cooking time:
2 hours
Serves 6

---

750 g minced beef
500 ml bottled
  spaghetti sauce
2 tablespoons finely
  chopped continental
  parsley
2 teaspoons finely
  chopped fresh mint
  leaves
1 clove garlic, crushed
salt and freshly
  ground black
  pepper, to taste

500 g packet tubular
  spaghetti
3 egg whites, lightly
  beaten

CHEESE TOPPING
100 g butter
1/2 cup plain flour
3 cups milk
3 egg yolks
1 cup grated cheddar
  cheese
1/4 cup packaged dry
  breadcrumbs

---

1 Preheat oven to moderate 180°C. Place mince in heavy-based pan. Stir constantly over high heat 10 minutes or until well browned and almost all liquid has evaporated. Use a fork to break up any lumps as it cooks. Add spaghetti sauce, herbs and garlic; bring to boil. Reduce heat and simmer, uncovered, for 30 minutes. Remove from heat, season to taste with salt and black pepper.

2 Cook pasta in large pan of boiling water until just tender; drain, rinse under cold water, drain again. Combine spaghetti with egg whites in a large mixing bowl.

3 To make Cheese Topping: Heat butter in medium pan; add flour. Stir over low heat 4 minutes or until flour mixture is lightly golden. Add milk gradually to pan, stirring until the mixture is smooth. Stir constantly over medium heat for 5 minutes or until mixture boils and thickens; boil further 1 minute; remove from heat. Cool to room temperature. Stir in egg yolks and grated cheese.

4 Spread half the spaghetti mixture over base of deep, greased baking dish. Cover with mince sauce, top with remaining spaghetti mixture. Pour cheese topping over, smooth surface. Sprinkle breadcrumbs over, bake 1 hour. Serve warm or cold.

Note: Add a little ground nutmeg to the cheese topping if liked. This dish can be frozen for up to one month. Reheat gently just before serving.

Cook mince until browned; add sauce, herbs and garlic to pan.

Cook pasta in a large pan of boiling water until just tender.

Remove flour mixture from heat and stir in egg yolks and cheese.

Assemble spaghetti mixture and mince in an ovenproof dish.

Lamb Parcels

Full of flavour.

Preparation time:
  30 minutes
Cooking time:
  35 minutes
Serves 6

---

6 (500 g) lamb fillets
3 tablespoons olive oil
2 small onions, sliced
2 slender eggplant,
   cut diagonally into
   thin slices
1 packet filo
   pastry
1/4 cup olive oil, extra
100 g feta or
   halloumi cheese
1/2 teaspoon dried
   rosemary

TOMATO HERB SAUCE
2 large ripe tomatoes,
   finely chopped
1 clove garlic, crushed
1 teaspoon dried
   oregano leaves
1 teaspoon fresh
   basil leaves
2 tablespoons red
   wine
1 teaspoon sugar

---

1 Preheat oven to moderate 180°C. Trim meat of excess fat and sinew. Heat 1 tablespoon of the olive oil in a frying pan, add onions and cook over medium heat for 4 minutes or until soft, stirring occasionally. Transfer onions to a plate, add 1 tablespoon oil to the pan and cook eggplant slices for 2 minutes each side, until just golden.

Drain on paper towel.
2 Heat remaining oil and cook meat in batches over high heat for 1 minute, until browned. Set aside to cool, then slice diagonally into 1 cm slices.
3 Lay a sheet of filo pastry on work surface, short side towards you. Brush lightly with olive oil, cover with another sheet, brush with oil, then top with one

more sheet. Place lamb in a rectangular pile about 10 cm in from short side of pastry, and 8 cm from each edge. Top with onions, eggplant, crumbled feta and rosemary. Fold short end of pastry over filling, fold the two long sides inward and roll up into a neat parcel. Brush with oil. Repeat with the remaining pastry and filling to make six parcels. Bake for 25 minutes until golden, serve with Tomato Herb Sauce.
4 To make Tomato Herb Sauce: Combine all ingredients in a small pan. Place over medium heat, bring to boil. Reduce heat slightly, simmer for 20 minutes until most liquid has evaporated, stirring occasionally. Serve warm.
Note: Cooked Tomato Herb Sauce may be added to the filling. Add sauce when making up parcels.

48

Cook eggplant slices for 2 minutes each side, until golden.

Brown meat and cut into diagonal strips 1 cm wide.

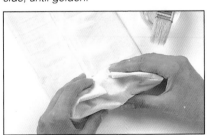

Fold pastry sides inward. Roll up into neat parcel.

Combine sauce ingredients in a small pan, simmer for 20 minutes.

Chicken with Okra

Preparation time:
 10 minutes
Cooking time:
 55 minutes
Serves 4

---

8 (750 g) chicken
 thigh cutlets
2 tablespoons butter,
 melted
2 cloves garlic,
 crushed
1/4 cup olive oil
2 large onions,
 thinly sliced

440 g can tomatoes,
 chopped
1/4 teaspoon ground
 black pepper
825 g can okra,
 drained, not rinsed

---

1 Trim chicken of excess fat and sinew. Place chicken on cold, lightly oiled grill tray. Cook under medium-high heat 12 minutes or until tender, turning once during cooking. Brush with combined butter and half the garlic several times during cooking. Remove from grill; keep warm.

2 Heat oil in heavy-based pan. Add onions and remaining garlic. Stir over high heat 3 minutes. Reduce heat to low, cook for a further 10 minutes, stirring occasionally. Add the tomatoes and pepper. Simmer, covered, for 5 minutes.

3 Preheat oven to moderately hot 210°C. Add okra to pan. Stir gently to combine. Simmer, covered, for 10 minutes. Pour okra mixture into shallow ovenproof dish.

4 Arrange chicken over okra. Bake for 15 minutes or until just heated through. Serve warm with bread, olives and cheese.

Note: Fresh okra can be used when in season. One kilo baby okra is sufficient for this recipe. Top and tail before cooking. Do not use large okra.

Place chicken on cold, lightly oiled grill tray. Cook until tender.

Heat oil in heavy-based pan and add onions and remaining garlic.

Stir in okra. Cover pan and simmer for 10 minutes.

Pour okra mixture into ovenproof dish. Arrange chicken pieces over.

Honey Lemon Chicken

Classic dish with a Greek touch.

Preparation time:
10 minutes
+ overnight
refrigeration
Cooking time:
45 minutes
Serves 4

---

1 kg chicken drumsticks	*1 teaspoon dried oregano*
1/4 cup olive oil	*4 cloves garlic, thinly sliced*
1/3 cup lemon juice	
1 tablespoon honey	*1 chicken stock cube, crumbled*
1 tablespoon dried rosemary	*2 teaspoons cornflour*
	1/2 cup water

---

1 Wipe and pat dry chicken with paper towel. Place chicken into a shallow dish. Combine oil, lemon, honey, herbs and garlic. Pour over the chicken. Cover with plastic wrap and refrigerate several hours or overnight, turning occasionally. Drain chicken and reserve marinade.

2 Preheat oven to moderate 180°C. Place chicken onto roasting rack over oven tray. Roast 30 minutes, turning once. Transfer to a shallow ovenproof dish; keep warm.

3 Combine any pan juices, reserved marinade and stock cube in a small pan.

4 Blend cornflour with water in small bowl until smooth; add to pan. Stir over medium heat 5 minutes or until sauce boils and thickens. Pour over chicken, return to oven, uncovered, for 10 minutes. Serve hot.

Note: Marinated chicken can also be grilled or barbecued. Baste occasionally with the reserved marinade during cooking. Use the remaining marinade to make sauce.

Combine oil, lemon, honey, herbs and garlic and pour over chicken.

Roast chicken on a rack over an oven tray, turning once during cooking.

Combine pan juices, marinade and stock cube in a small pan.

Blend cornflour and water until smooth and add to pan.

53

Chicken with Cauliflower and Cinnamon

Preparation time:
20 minutes +
2 hours standing
Cooking time:
1 hour 10 minutes
Serves 4

---

8 (750 g) chicken wings
750 g cauliflower
3/4 cup dry red wine
1 tablespoon tomato paste
3/4 cup rich chicken stock

1/2 teaspoon ground cinnamon
1/2 teaspoon ground black pepper
salt, to taste
1/3 cup olive oil

---

1 Wipe and pat dry chicken wings with paper towel. Tuck the wing tips to underside. Place chicken into a large bowl. Cut cauliflower into 12 large florets. Add to bowl with the chicken.

2 Combine wine and tomato paste in a small bowl. Pour over chicken and cauliflower. Store, covered with plastic wrap, in refrigerator for 2 hours, turning occasionally.

3 Preheat oven to moderately hot 210°C. Transfer the chicken, cauliflower and marinade to a deep baking dish. Place stock, cinnamon, pepper, salt and oil in small bowl, beat 2 minutes or until well combined. Pour over ingredients in dish.

4 Bake, uncovered, for 1 hour, turning occasionally. Transfer the chicken and cauliflower to serving dish using a slotted spoon or tongs. Keep warm. Transfer pan to stove top and heat pan juices over high heat 5 minutes, stirring constantly. Cook until mixture reduces and thickens slightly. Season to taste, pour over chicken and cauliflower. Serve hot.

Wipe and pat dry chicken wings. Tuck wing tips to underside.

Combine the red wine and tomato paste and mix well.

Pour the wine mixture over chicken and cauliflower.

Bake chicken with marinade, stock, cinnamon, pepper, salt and oil.

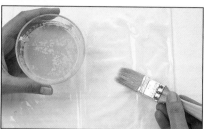

Brush half a sheet of filo with combined butter and oil. Fold in half widthways.

Sprinkle one portion of walnut mixture over pastry in dish.

Cut the slice evenly into four, without cutting right through.

Remove baklava from oven and pour cool syrup over the hot pastry.

SWEETS

Whether packed with nuts or dusted with icing sugar, the sweet things from Greece are equally delicious.

Baklava

Spices, filo and nuts.

Preparation time:
15 minutes
Cooking time:
30 minutes
Serves 4–6

375 g (3 1/2 cups) walnuts, finely chopped, not ground
160 g (1 cup) almonds, finely chopped
1/2 teaspoon ground cinnamon
1/2 teaspoon ground mixed spice
1 tablespoon caster sugar

16 sheets filo pastry
2 tablespoons butter, melted
1 tablespoon olive oil

SYRUP
1 cup sugar
2/3 cup water
3 whole cloves
3 teaspoons lemon juice

1 Preheat oven to moderate 180°C. Brush the sides and base of a shallow 18 x 28 cm ovenproof dish with melted butter or oil. Combine walnuts, almonds, spices and sugar in medium bowl; divide into three portions. Place one sheet of pastry onto work surface. Brush half the sheet with combined butter and oil mixture; fold in half widthways. Trim edges to fit dish. Place into base of prepared dish. Repeat process with another three sheets of pastry.

2 Sprinkle one portion of walnut mixture over pastry. Repeat pastry process with four more sheets. Sprinkle with second portion of walnut mixture. Continue with another four sheets of pastry, remaining walnut mixture and final four sheets of pastry. Trim edges.

3 Brush top of pastry with remaining butter and oil mixture. Cut the slice evenly into four lengthways. (Do not cut through to the base.) Bake for 30 minutes or until golden and crisp.

4 Pour cooled syrup over hot slice. When cold, cut slice into squares or diamonds.

5 To make Syrup: Combine ingredients in small pan. Stir constantly over low heat until mixture boils and sugar has dissolved. Reduce heat, simmer, without stirring, for 10 minutes.

Sweet Custard Rolls

Vanilla custard in filo pastry.

Preparation time:
15 minutes +
10 minutes
standing
Cooking time:
50 minutes
Serves 6–8

---

1 lemon	14 sheets filo pastry
3 cups milk	2 tablespoons
1/2 cup coarse	unsalted butter,
semolina	melted
1/4 cup rice flour	1 tablespoon oil
2/3 cup caster sugar	2 tablespoons icing
2 eggs, lightly beaten	sugar
1 teaspoon vanilla	1/2 teaspoon ground
essence	cinnamon

---

1 Grease a 32 x 28 cm oven tray. Peel lemon rind into three strips 1 x 5 cm long. Combine rind with milk in small heavy-based pan. Stir over low heat until almost boiling. Reduce heat and simmer, covered, 10 minutes. Remove pan from heat; leave to cool for 10 minutes. Remove peel.

2 Using electric beaters, beat semolina, rice flour, sugar and eggs on low speed 2 minutes or until smooth. Add milk gradually, beating thoroughly after each addition. Return mixture to pan. Stir over medium heat 10 minutes or until mixture boils and thickens. Remove custard from heat, stir in essence.

3 Cover surface of custard with plastic wrap to prevent skin forming, allow to cool. Preheat oven to moderate 180°C. Place all the sheets of pastry onto the work surface. Using a sharp knife or scissors, cut filo widthways into three even pieces. Brush one piece with combined butter and oil, top with a second piece. Brush one narrow end with butter mixture.

4 Place 2 tablespoons of custard 2 cm in from opposite end. Roll pastry over filling. Fold ends in towards filling; roll to end of pastry. Repeat with remaining pastry and custard. Arrange rolls onto prepared tray about 2 cm apart. Brush with remaining butter mixture. Bake 30 minutes or until pastry is puffed and lightly golden. Serve warm, dusted with combined icing sugar and cinnamon.

Note: While working, keep filo pastry covered with a clean damp cloth to prevent sheets drying out. Cover the assembled rolls to prevent the pastry drying.

Peel the lemon rind into three strips, each 5 cm long.

Add the cooled milk gradually to the semolina mixture.

Cover surface of custard with plastic wrap to prevent a skin forming.

Place 2 tablespoons of custard on one end of filo and roll pastry over filling.

Coconut Semolina Syrup Cake

Preparation time:
30 minutes
Cooking time:
1 hour
Serves 6–8

---

250 g unsalted butter
1 cup caster sugar
3 eggs, lightly beaten
1 teaspoon vanilla
essence
1 cup fine ground
semolina
3/4 cup desiccated
coconut

1 1/4 cups self-raising
flour

LEMON SYRUP
3/4 cup sugar
1 cup water
1 lemon, thinly sliced

---

1 Preheat oven to moderate 180°C. Brush a deep 23 cm springform tin with melted butter or oil. Line base and sides with paper; grease paper. Using electric beaters, beat butter and sugar in small mixing bowl for 10 minutes. Add eggs gradually, beating thoroughly after each addition. Add essence and semolina; beat 5 minutes.

2 Transfer mixture to large mixing bowl; add coconut. Using a metal spoon, fold in sifted flour. Stir until just combined and mixture is smooth.

3 Spoon mixture evenly into prepared tin; smooth surface. Bake 1 hour or until a skewer comes out clean when inserted in centre of cake. Pour cold syrup over hot cake in pan. When cold, remove paper. Serve cake with the lemon slices and cream.

4 To make Lemon Syrup: Combine sugar and water in small pan. Stir constantly over low heat until mixture boils and sugar has dissolved; add lemon. Bring to boil, reduce heat and simmer, uncovered, without stirring 15 minutes.

Beat butter and sugar together. Add eggs gradually, beating well.

Using a metal spoon, fold the sifted flour into the well-beaten semolina mixture.

Bake for 1 hour or until a skewer comes out clean when inserted in cake.

Add lemon slices to syrup mixture. Simmer 15 minutes without stirring.

Greek Shortbread

Preparation time:
20 minutes
Cooking time:
25 minutes
Makes 24

---

250 g unsalted butter
1/2 cup icing sugar, sifted
1 egg yolk
1 teaspoon vanilla essence
1 tablespoon brandy

3/4 cup roasted hazelnuts, finely chopped
1 teaspoon baking powder
3 cups plain flour, sifted
1 cup icing sugar, extra

---

1 Preheat oven to moderate 180°C. Using electric beaters, beat butter and sugar in small mixing bowl until light and creamy. Add yolk, beat well. Add vanilla essence and brandy; beat until combined.
2 Transfer mixture to large mixing bowl; add nuts, baking powder and flour. Working quickly, use hands to press ingredients together to form a soft dough. Do not knead.
3 Shape 2 tablespoons of mixture at a time into a crescent shape.

Repeat with the remaining mixture. Place crescents onto ungreased biscuit tray about 4 cm apart. Bake 25 minutes or until lightly golden. Remove, cool on tray.
4 When cool, dust crescents liberally with icing sugar. Serve shortbread with Greek coffee. **Note:** If the mixture is too soft to handle, use lightly floured hands to shape dough into crescents. Substitute finely chopped roasted walnuts for hazelnuts in this recipe if liked. In Greece, desserts or sweets are traditionally served an hour after dinner, with coffee.

Using electric beaters, beat butter and sugar until light and creamy.

Working quickly, use hands to press ingredients together to form a soft dough.

Shape 2 tablespoons of mixture at a time into a crescent shape.

Dust cooked, cooled shortbread liberally with icing sugar.

INDEX